IN THE ANTARCTIC CIRCLE

WINNER OF THE
2020 AUTUMN HOUSE
RISING WRITER PRIZE

IN THE ANTARCTIC CIRCLE

DENNIS JAMES SWEENEY

AUTUMN
HOUSE PRESS

Autumn House Press receives state arts funding support through a grant from the Pennsylvania Council on the Arts, a state agency funded by the Commonwealth of Pennsylvania, and the National Endowment for the Arts, a federal agency.

ISBN: 978-1-938769-72-6
Library of Congress Control Number: 2020947413

Cover illustration: Malte Mueller / Getty Images
Book & cover design: Joel W. Coggins

All Autumn House books are printed on acid-free paper and meet the international standards of permanent books intended for purchase by libraries.

IN THE ANTARCTIC CIRCLE

In this Antarctica, there is no unemployment, there is no indigence, and the crime rate is negligible. The air is the cleanest in the world. Medical care and literacy are universal. The cost of living is possibly the highest in the world but, at least in the case of National Antarctic Programs, heavily subsidized by the state. Antarctica seems a wholly elite space—gazed upon only by a privileged few—a place of vast and terrible white emptiness where history might be written *tabula rasa* by Great (White) Men.

—Lize-Marié van der Watt and Sandra Swart

He and I walk through a forest. Trees black. Leaves red. Moon orange and viscous like a yolk in hair. Around a corner our car appears with headlights furrowed, growling.

At home, we count foodstuffs. Months stretch like limbs into the limbless night. The smell of forest on him freezes under ice, a thin sheet meant to preserve the body but only halting it.

The bed yawns under us. He and I grip fingers. Thighs on thighs like batons. Do not say the word out loud.

I can feel the continent dragging cold toes to us. I pull the blanket over us, remembering again the trees. Shadows of trees. The forest, whether it was there. Our feet like bones wrapped in bones. Image of land rising to meet us, desperate awaiting. But when it meets us it is not land.

We live together in flight, he and I. I can already feel.

The white ice sheet cracking. We are on it or it is on us or it goes through us, which I believe is the most likely case. It knows the facts of us insofar as it erases them. On either side, blue organs, breathing and lost.

The shoreless infinity of loss, which no one knows until they have lost themselves. I have surrendered myself to a vision of days ahead. Blank place to place a foot. Lush seconds drowned under the mindless crystal stretch. Light locked below zero.

I take a step. I am as aware as my body's last sensation. The remainder of the steps will take themselves.

And now we rushed into the embraces of the cataract, where
a chasm threw itself open to receive us. But there arose in our
pathway a shrouded human figure, very far larger in its proportions
than any dweller among men. And the hue of the skin of the figure
was of the perfect whiteness of the snow.

—Edgar Allan Poe

Whiteness, alone, is mute, meaningless, unfathomable, pointless,
frozen, veiled, curtained, dreaded, senseless, implacable. Or so our
writers seem to say.

—Toni Morrison

74°0′S 108°30′W

Scan the snow for objects of love and wonder. Boil seal meat, stirring with both arms. Keep the bed unmade so it cannot be forgotten that each day is a new day under the ever-rising sun: God forbid the sheets keep their creases. God forbid an inch of sanitation tiptoe in. Wrestle your urges to the ground and gut them. The snow outside the front door turns a merciful red.

66°30′S 109°30′E

Six birds emerge, trailing bleach, from the ocean.

Everything was dead.

We laugh and laugh and laugh.

Memory is there somewhere.

And red leaves.

The shore crawls slowly away, but I know a man who will bring it back.

Leashes will be used. Dredges.

Today, the living are marking what they can.

67°55′S 44°38′E

What we do, we do as scientists: take/give back, take/give back until everything has wound its way through us. Cut out negative space. Tie flags around the birds. It's simple, habitation, as long as you keep your finger on the dial. Sensitive as a nipple. In the cold, everything is harder to know.

Which is why we venture out, day after day.

Why the shadows know which way to run.

In every direction, miniatures of our bodies poke from the snow. We placed them there. Aspiring Edvard Munches.

Paint the snow with white paint. Not yet white enough. Not yet the color of the backs of the eyes, removed.

66°20′S 124°38′E

When you find us, we will strip off your parka and drag you out into the snow and bury you there with only your head in the wind.

You will learn: Negative sixty degrees is not absolute zero.

You will learn: In a whiteout you cannot see shadows, but that does not mean the edges are not there.

Sastrugi form over your face. In seconds you are a desert, evacuated, the living watching from a distance with their cheeks in their hands.

We will treat you like a god, but you have to find us first. We're not as far away as you think.

74°50′S 132°0′W

When we were kids, black plastic paved the walls.

We hunted darkness.

Hank fingered my hand in the exacting night.

Like creatures. Flashes.

We believed we had seen ghosts.

There was no history.

Antarctica was ten thousand white hairs.

That stood and shook—and in the bright of sleep, inched into our breathing beds.

THIS PAGE
INTENTIONALLY
LEFT BLANK

I long to see a lemonade stand setting up at the crossroads. Hell, I long to see a crossroads. Children waving a hand-painted sign in the hope that—

The hope—

It has no substance yet.

I would be cruel to wish this place on children. I wish for it anyway. The landform is a lesson in consequence, in the fact that stars and snow and wind know nothing of you except that you block their way.

Then fly the kids back. Television. Peanuts. Jet fuel leaking into the burners. Their milk-white minds searing the bone-white sky. And Hank and I, unbeknownst to all, hanging on to the landing gear as it pulls up.

72°3′S 102°20′W

Harpoons loll in our arms like children too old to be held. Along the horizon animals run, disappearing over the brink of snow.

A few toddly steps after them. Our own animal horizon.

Black toboggans of the future.

Christmas upside-down in the lake.

The white arms-and-legs hunch in accidental shelters, newly troubled by the color orange.

Their tracks fill up, making time. The sky continues to do what little it can.

70°40′S 8°16′W

Maybe you can build something, even in the snow. Maybe I can kiss your cracked hand. Maybe we can rise at noon and eat gingersnaps out of the bag.

I know, I know. The hard part is yet to come.

The stars are not what we thought they would be. With mittens you can't point at constellations, can't trace a figure between the specks. Before we've guessed at a single story, the sky is purple all at once, then green, and we're rushing inside to slowly thaw.

We change colors too, but only in relation to one another. There are some slow truths. Biding their time as we make up games to pass the winter: War, Skirmish, Tear The Tissue Into Tinier And Tinier Bits.

War is what I mean when I say we change color. Blood on the floor, deranged proposals with harpoon held aloft. Coffee table without coffee. Shrill numbing light.

66°27′S 91°54′E

Your big red hood is up. Your vision an oval framed in fur. You wear kilograms of clothing. You manhandle the winter. Tear organs from its open stomach, melt them down and eat them. The wind sneaks past. Times are sharp. You see fog. You must be still. You wait out eternities. You have to remember that the outside does not get tired. Only you. Put your altruism away. First the pancreas, then the liver. Full of winter's bitter fat.

76°58′S 148°45′W

Hank is a man tangled up in the fibers of what he once believed.

Example: Take a crummy fork and set it on the table instead of leaning it on your dish.

Example: Bear the loneliness longer than you can stand.

Hank sweeps in, underwear over outerwear, and prevents your dreams from becoming soiled. Raises the fork from the table before the germs have a chance to grab on. Discourses at length on seclusion, which is really just a state of mind.

He fancies himself a man's man. Waves his sword. Treasures blood on it. Doesn't know he's not the only one who doesn't want to be saved.

THIS PAGE

INTENTIONALLY

HINTS AT LOSS

70°45′S 11°38′E

You can't hope without certainty. Trust me, I know. The battlements are the color of longing, which is the color of knowing that no one is coming home.

A set of keys that will work on *something*.

A miracle inching toward you on its hands and knees.

Frozen, the air is less turbulent to travel. Messages wing recklessly across Antarctica.

Everyone is convinced that nothing will shift, save for the restless penguins that waddle the horizon. This is not a place of change. It is a place of open eyes. A place of sun off snow. Of breath held.

Though no savior is due, we make a life of waiting. Everyone has every reason to fold.

75°30′S 107°0′W

Breed me. Make me new with snow. Hank, mold my eyes.

Dishware in white.

The idea of thorns.

Something to protect.

Harmony is a sort of absence. Following what's left.

We have discovered: No matter how many animals we kill they barely run, knowing they cannot be shaped by anyone else's want.

A heart is too found to run through.

Arrive—

The blizzard mourns fully and gently over you.

64°54′S 63°37′W

The stranger makes his approach on the long beach of the polar cap.
He raises a hand. You wrinkle at him. What does he want from you?

All you want from him is that hand, severed, in a bag of ice to bring
home and keep at the side of your bed. You know what Hank would
say: Hand! I'll give you a hand! And drag his palm across the floor.
He'd lift it and it would be dust.

Just my luck. I haven't swept for a lifetime.

Instead, you stare at the stranger until his body has dissolved into a
thousand hanging beads of ice.

Disillusionment is easy.

I would rather bite another man's fingernails than stop.

74°45′S 120°0′W

Antarctica left me head-down in the snow, counting days for men who would not fly. The hard-heeled tap-on-ice. The somber household refrain: *Be gone, little beast, and leave me to my fear.* But not for long. Buy a serum. Buy a side of beef. Buy sandbags. His corona is already beginning to leak.

77°0′S 152°30′W

I remember the time when you were beached.

Hank, hold the whistle.

I stepped gingerly across the ice toward you as it cracked.

Our kids would never wear floaties.

Our kids would not know the word *milk*.

Certainly something to fear—the inevitable drift, the way the ocean forever washes in and takes you up and returns you to from where you came. Without ever shushing to ask.

I am alone in the whiteness. I stretch into it and huddle.

The sorry is so terribly wide.

----

*THIS PAGE
REVOKES ALL
OTHER PAGES*

72°45′S 88°50′W

You need a dread in a place like this, something more than ornery tradition clawing up the walls.

Ours is fungus. It doesn't grow—nothing grows, this is Antarctica—but we like to make believe. Hank drops a spatula and I shriek at him to pick it up. The mold is setting in! I say. They've got us by the tongue!

If I stay in one spot long enough, I can feel the mushrooms growing on my knees, tight gray flecks of information preparing for a rain that will never come. They thirst and scrape. The image gets me out of the chair, off the floor.

Hank was mycophobic, back on land. There's plenty of room for phobias here.

I keep trying for deathly afraid, but I'm failing. I used to pray for distant relatives to expire for the simple sake of crisis. Now I hope aloud for mildew.

The Antarctic Circle, cold and blithe, shrugs. Its shoulders evaporate into the sky.

69°45′S 39°5′E

Translation: Put your oar down and come with me.

Translation: This is not an open city.

Translation: The bar is closed, we've all gone home, we've got lives. Do you have a life? The keg is in the corner wrapped in a fishing net, the bar is closed.

Translation: The way home is precisely the distance between you and the horizon.

Translation: Everyone is barefoot by now.

Translation: Except you.

71°35′S 0°30′E

How Hank got his harpoon back from the sea. Whether blood stains ice. Just the sheer size of those creatures. The sheer -*ness*, as approached by lies.

The way the bear wriggled in its skin as it died, wanting to be as loose as us. The box of the sky. More weight than we could drag a half-mile.

Ice, not as slippery as you would think.

We hold our wounds dear, open them repeatedly, sell them for further wounds, trap the blood in cycles of sighing. Men, we keep calling ourselves, because I insist.

In wellness, we wait for the coming storm. Our rites of love and boredom circle each other, waving their leather whips.

SNOW: A DEFINITION

1. Snow.
2. A definition.
3. Your mother is saying goodbye to you.
4. White.
5. Every human will be miserable for ____ of their life.
6. What good is this?
7. What use for the long heart?
8. Prayer.
9. *Memento mori*; or, simply, bones.
10. Tracks in the ____.
11. Tip of the fingernail.
12. Happiness; or, mirror; or, a car alarm at four in the morning, waking you from a dream of splitting ice.
13. Tears in the newborn.
14. Tears in the elderly.
15. Cocaine.
16. The flying machine leaves at ____.
17. Calculate chances of ____.
18. Young men pursue a couch through a storm, grin at the camera, toast to health.
19. The cat house.
20. The bat house.
21. ____, hot fear.
22. Emptiness.
23. The color of weight; or, of wait.
24. Tender armies.
25. A silent attempt at adventure.
26. Old film.
27. New film with romantic aspirations.
28. "Peace Studies."

29. Across the country, people moan in pleasure while you lie naked in your room waiting for the ceiling to fall on you, which is _____.
30. Narnia; or, Mordor; or, England; or, the sewer; or, home.
31. Tiny, flying corks.
32. "Truth-telling."
33. "Always-already."
34. An amalgamation of ancients.
35. _____.
36. A cover, to anything.
37. The contours of the hills where your mother was given her maiden name; or, where she lost it.
38. Soft and fine.
39. Gravity for the robes.
40. A ring of _____ around the more precious metals.
41. Repeat.
42. Someone's hair.
43. Believe in what will die before you will.
44. *Sans* milk, *sans* breast.
45. "Chrome."
46. The freezer section for more than a year, with a mop.
47. The fourth cross.
48. Invisible hand, invisible nail.
49. Chicagoland.
50. The process of forgetting to forget.

THIS PAGE

IS A WALL

AN OBLITERATION

A STEP

67°31′S 61°37′E

Let's suppose the world never ends. Let's suppose we're here into perpetuity, cooling heels at the rim of the great gone-cold hot tub. I throw in the towel. It begins to sink. Hank dives in, reaching one heroic hand out of the water where he's drowning, the towel clutched in it. Soaked. Drying for only a moment before his weight pulls it down to the bottom.

We enact the cycles. We buy in, whether we want to or not, to biotic recursion, watersheds, the boogaloo. But we haven't forgotten silence, not with as much armchair in front of us as we've got. The silence doesn't circle. Rather lurks, impatient, then jumps on whatever slows.

Hank doesn't need a warning, though today the weather did. The clouds began to settle above us and I told them the hard truth: It's for your sake that I ask you to move on.

They gave up, as I hoped they would. No reason to dance their white dance on white.

Hank has his own way of coping. Takes the silence before it takes him. He's like a dog bounding through a field of bones. Human bones, nothing the dog ought to like. But he does. He can't help it. You can either love the whole world or push it away from you, and the dog is hungry. Hank will chew on anything that smells like it was once alive.

62°57′S 60°38′W

The latitude and longitude of my love—etc., etc.

You can't map emptiness. Only affiliations.

One day we will be trampled by the exodus, millions of lives dragging their cities behind them, breaking windows on the ice, tumbling into the ocean.

Skyscrapers as icebergs. Crumbling apartments as polar caps.

Something to stand on, to wave from to the saviors.

Who're coming soon, you have to believe. The vacant landscape— white, silent, etc.—knows nothing less than endless faith.

66°12′S 136°11′E

Creation is a weather map. The background—studio lighting, an electrical hum—stretches wide, wide.

Mash your eyes with fingers and you can almost hear the anchors chatter about their home lives, the children who hate them, the clouds that won't quit dancing above their pool dates and raising goosebumps on their skin. They are naked and the cameras show everything.

As night falls, the shot pans gradually away and we are only a green screen behind the news desk, a placeholder for the unsung attraction between our companions.

We wait eagerly for their return. We long to show them the heavy mystery of their ignorance but the next day is a holiday, and the day after that.

Flat and cold, we wait.

None of the other inanimate objects know us. The stars, shining down from rails stretched across the ceiling, whisper further truths. But the microphones are tiny, tiny. Play the whispers back and they sound like waves licking a hunched pattern of rocks and the land, safe from the water, laughing.

77°8′S 154°0′W

We cut holes in the ice and sip history out of it. Afterward, they weigh us. The scale doesn't register. They tag our ears and send us back.

No loss to us. Our steps are lighter underneath the past. The snow gives less, has less to give.

At home, the dome cradles us back into our short ugly memories. The ancient lies rise and gather blackly at the ceiling.

We can't help but cower. Our fathers are there somewhere, breathing hard.

Their voices are magnets. Our voices are echoes, kindling fame.

69°45′S 71°0′E

I've been waking myself through the inestimable power of boredom. Dream and dream until the field is empty, until nothing waddles toward you or throws up its hands, until the clouds remain mute against a featureless horizon.

The world has less to offer than you think. A few chores, the distinct pleasure of not-knowing, then you're back to lying spread-eagle in the snow at the massive, slow threat of geological time. Maybe a bear comes up and sniffs you. Maybe a bird pecks at your chest and reminds you there's such a thing as grocery stores, produce aisles lined with flags of underripe fruit.

We'll return when it's time to return. Until then, keep your eyes trained on something. The long cut of a jet stream between two sections of sky. A fleck of dirt stuck to your jumpsuit, in flight from the permafrost a thousand miles to the north. In a year, it—you— God! everything!—will be white.

THIS PAGE
IS WITHOUT
THE FEATURES
OF A PAGE
AND YET

70°5'S 65°40'E

In the Antarctic Circle, our main concern is self-husbandry. Cutting dark chops from the dark sky. Identifying lifelong manacles. Feeling for the key.

Suspending paper katydids from the ceiling at just the right angle: the difference between Hank's breath and the hot, light breeze of the radiator. They trigger different flights. At times you can't tell whether the wings are held aloft by a string from the ceiling or whether the house is held together by the wings, all through the string.

Other points are moot as yet. We wander out each day. Death is far from the question.

76°50′S 155°0′W

The old world ran with unpredictable dogs.

The old world was once the new world. We stumbled across ourselves. Found them completely naked.

Memories of hay fever. Of uneven sidewalks. Of a garden hose shattering the air.

No in and no out. No hierarchy. No beginning or end.

A soggy newspaper spread on the kitchen floor.

Brittle boxes of cereal.

71°15′S 163°0′E

The vans escorted the unwanted to the farthest reaches and dropped us off. On the far horizon were white craniums bursting from the snow: our homes. On the near horizon, the hard-faced drivers dipped and disappeared.

We were alone. Nine gave in, eventually, to the cold. Two of us survived, warmed as we were by witlessness.

We lowered our heads. We pretended there was no wind.

Soon enough there wasn't. Inside the plaster cranium, we cast about for warmth. I swayed in my parka. He beat his thighs to bring back blood. Then we recognized: Spread on the carpetless floors were the accoutrements of our former lives.

The furniture was both of ours, although I had never seen his face. He unwrapped the wool from his neck, his mouth.

His name was Hank, he said, holding out his hand.

Mine, I said, was mine.

A similar logic underlies the Antarctic Treaty System itself, which declares Antarctica "the continent for science and peace," forbids any military presence (except to support scientific activities), suspends the possibility of mining and protects the environment. After the 1991 Madrid Protocol, strict regulations were placed on the bringing of foreign organisms into the Antarctic regions. Human visitors are required to remove all waste they produce. Antarctica's unstable borders are now policed like no other continent's.

—Elizabeth Leane

Antarctica is thus the most-mediated, manipulated, surveilled territory on the planet.

—Elena Glasberg

It wouldn't be right to call these found documents. It wouldn't be right to call them documents at all, seeing as I came upon them carved into the snow on my last day in Antarctica, where I stayed for the two years following my divorce. People asked, "Don't you want to leave?" People told me, "You have to leave. There is a whole world." Only after they stopped speaking to me altogether did I reach the limit of blankness, an opaque white threshold, and call the American base to ready the warm belly of their C-130 Hercules for one further passenger, a cold one, a person who had for a long time not even attempted to get warm.

By that time, I had made myself indispensable to those geologists whose goal was to collect meteorites that fell on the fresh snow of the continent. I had wandered into their blue tents one day—this is how they describe it, although I don't recall arriving—and asked for shelter. The rule here is that you give when asked. I stayed for seven days curled by a heat lamp, staring at them as they donned their jumpsuits and goggles and charms they strung around their necks or wrists or stuck in their pockets. The tent flap opened. They disappeared. An incalculable time later, they appeared again carrying sealed plastic bags under their arms. I watched with something akin to hunger. Then, on the morning of the eighth day, I stood and told the scientists I was ready to accompany them. They were so taken aback to hear me speak that, inadvisably, they let me. Someone pulled out the extra jumpsuit and a pair of cracked goggles, and I followed the crew out into the snow.

I watched them roam in precise geometrical patterns across the white plain, bending occasionally to look at the ground before shaking their heads and straightening again. Only twice in the course of three hours did they find something. The victorious scientist held up a bulging bag and whooped. The others yipped across the ice's silence. Then they fell into their pattern again.

In the fourth hour of their search, I set to looking. In that hour I found seventeen pieces of interstellar debris. I simply walked from one to the next, following no pattern I could discern. Sometimes I sensed a speck from as far as a hundred yards away. I'd walk to it, pick it up. The scientists would rush to the spot. By the end of the hour the entire crew was following me, hunched in the shadows of my footsteps, struggling to see how I saw what I did.

It was not long, as I said, before I grew indispensable. I found meteorites the way a dog finds shit, one of the men liked to claim, and I was not yet sufficiently reattuned to the contingencies of conversation to hear an insult in what he said. I suffered some amnesia after my divorce, I mean to say. It was strange the things I did not remember and the things I became able to do.

The geologists made a bed for me, and a shelf, and a space in the hole in the snow outside they called the fridge. The arrangement seemed natural. I woke, they followed me, I pointed to the dust of stars, they picked it up. Every couple of days someone would gather up the plastic baggies we had stacked beside the doorway. A snowmobile's engine would kick to life, then fade. I gathered that the specks I found were prized, but never that I was prized. Something in me halted before the breadth of the idea that I might be able to contribute.

Two years passed this way. Scientists came and went. "You need a rest," they said, as only the most seasoned hands lived on the continent for an entire calendar year. But I stayed, and I showed no signs of waning health. My vision had even improved. My eyes, they muttered, were green, glowing, wild. I did not take this personally. I considered the eyes to be quite separate from me.

Every day I went out. Every day I discovered more space material, in this sector and that, and the horizonless expanse continued to work on me. Although I was always walking toward a thing, that thing was always finally removed from its pock in the snow and it was up to me to find something new. I did so. But the endless nature of the plain sent me barreling forward into an unprecedented experience of blankness.

Emptiness is a romantic idea for some people. For me it was the only remaining way of life.

On that day when I reached the limit—how did I know? how does a baby know it's born?—the scientists were assiduously silent toward me. The light had drained from my eyes, I felt, and entered my icy limbs. I slipped into my tattered jumpsuit. I folded back the door of the tent. I wandered out into the snow alone. I wandered for a long time, though there were no meteorites left to find. There were only these words inscribed in the distance.

They were written into the continent between long swaths of white. I followed and followed. There was ice, the empty sky. There were words, and I wrote them down.

I wish I could take you on to the great Ice Barrier some calm evening
when the sun is just dipping in the middle of the night and show you
the autumn tints on Ross Island. A last look round before turning in,
a good day's march behind, enough fine fat pemmican inside you
to make you happy, the homely smell of tobacco from the tent, a
pleasant sense of soft fur and the deep sleep to come. And all the
softest colours God has made are in the snow. . .

—Apsley Cherry-Garrard

62°27′S 60°20′W

He holds the walls apart, his head pressing in, my head emptying of matter.

He pulls my shoulders back to where they belong.

He sets a pot on the stove and sits beside me. Holding our hands in our laps, we watch it freeze.

The sky's green lights are us, on fire.

Small miracles of domesticity lie flat on the unspotted plain.

The end that can be reached is not the true end.

Our home is your margin.

God bless you.

Take this:

68°35'S 77°58'E

By August, the fat has begun to drip away. Infants cry in the distance. We hold it together by singing laments for love and loss in a land that has never known either. We storm the grated pathways with all the heart we would otherwise fuck with. We throw forbidding glances at those men who can be seen through their beards. Don't touch me. Wave your instruments at the stars. Whatever you do, confine your dreams to the unanswerable because I am farther away even than those points of light. If the snow calls to you, fuck it. Strip to the skin and let the flakes burn you until you are blue.

63°22′S 56°58′W

I want the same things we all want. A place to build a fire, something to burn, something to warm in the heat, something to put in my mouth. A secure stance on hard ground. Nothing too quickly to melt.

Dear God: I have everything.

Then again, what about the hunt? What about the game that has fled at our human angles, at our shadows that lengthen across the snow? What about blood?

I haven't bled since arriving.

Hank hasn't noticed. I taste his fear.

Of what is in me that bleeds, rather than what is out of me and will certainly kill.

Of a life preparing. Blankness, too, can gestate. In the halt it has begun.

THIS PAGE
IS WHERE
WE AREN'T,
TOGETHER

70°45′S 12°30′E

I'm there now—no longer here—and the people treat me like I am one of them.

Their satchels are full. They are always bringing something somewhere. I am jealous, and they do not know how to steal.

Easy: Take what you want and fall on it like a grenade.

See? The stakes are different here in that every ridge, every barely shining spur, is a handle. It goes unsaid between Hank and me that the barest discrepancy owes a full report. Unless it's toenails. Ten every time we snip. We don't want to lay our mechanisms so bare.

What I was saying: You can't treat a diversion too good. So I keep eyes closed.

Dangle my feet from the horizon. Then when night comes it is unquestionably our night.

NOTHING: A DEFINITION

n. v. adv. adj. prep. pron. conj. Tear. ( ). Miracle. Men. Grasping. "Ghost." Profound-er. Particle. Blanket. Sheath. Margin. Total. Body: flee. Target. Miss-ter. Blink-er. Tank-er. Particle. Switz-er(-land). *int.! int.!* Law. Participle. A child (rearing). Blind-er. Major, unsung. What is there under a rock? Wheel well. Pinpoints. Connect the _____. Tranquiliz-er. Business. Particle. Hero. Garment. Wine, water, air. _____ crawls across you for all time, leaving its claws in _____. Particle. Heart. Expansion set. Hadrian. Mast-er. Distance between *in* and *on* the wall. Cold and certain. "Ice." Memory. Particle. Carve a mortar and pestle. Climb a tree. Release a child from your whim and look down.

70°38′S 71°58′E

Hank would put on a dress for me. He'd pierce his ears. He'd walk out in the snow barefoot and wait for the flurries to take him.

They never will. I never will either.

Thoughts congeal up there and they never come down.

Instead of rapture, he'll bring back a wing he found disembodied on the swath and we'll put it on the table between us and stare at it for an hour.

The common disaffection—dishes, hair on the carpet—is a relief after something like that. You have to keep reminding yourself that the honeymoon is never over. No matter how you hide, it crawls back to you.

When it returns, it is in the form of impossible flight. Of a single wing snapped from the lost body of a tern.

74°15′S 125°0′W

Time stands still. Time contracts. Time follows you to the toilet. Time brushes his teeth. Time spits in the sink and begins to floss. Everything is quiet. You can hear the dental tape in time's gums pulling out pieces of dinner. Plaque slaps against the mirror. Time glances at you on the toilet. Time turns the faucet on. He runs the water until you can't stand it anymore. Then you realize he is doing it for you. So you can pee in anonymity. Time leaves the bathroom. Time leaves the faucet on. Time leaves the door open. Time stands right outside, cracking his naked toes.

75°14′S 45°45′W

Our story is the story of ten thousand men and a sprinkler system and a sudden freeze. Our story is the story of a cowlick gone to heaven and punished there. Our story halts outside the gates, wraps its fingers around the gates, is arrested for protesting the gates, is bailed out by its rich mother.

Our story grows facial hair, inch by inch. Sirens gaze out from between the strands of our wandering beards.

It is best not to shave, Hank and I agree. Something inside is wailing. That thing can wait. *Should* wait. It knows us like the cold knows the back of our necks.

THIS PAGE
HOLDS A PAGE
NAMED AFTER IT
WITH NO NAME

73°30'S 96°0'W

Hand over hand into benefit of the doubt, we swim through the black cloud of dishes undone and underwear on the bed. But the space is small. No room for triumph when you have to duck to get out the door.

Like hauling an elephant seal into the living room and gutting it. Like trying to dwell in its stomach. We could spread its guts on the plaster, paint the walls with blood, but where would that leave us? Under the watchful eye of rotlessness. Permanent art installation. Too cold even for a mistake to right itself.

The way things are going, I'd drown myself in ice in a minute. Then I'd be stuck, free from the passing time.

Someday, I dream, the ice will melt long enough to support immersion. Some night, the borealis will fall to us.

FOR THOSE WHO HAVE NO PREFERENCES

*

I am a vestibule for emptiness.

I am a land built on fat promises.

I am a dull paring knife.

I am bludgeoning frozen fruit.

I am saddled with saintliness.

Escorted out the fire door.

A cactus in the tundra.

The tundra in a cactus.

The worn rug beneath the man of integrity.

I am the last mile.

You are the first circumference.

*

A Madonna holds a cat like a gun.

Mirage of superfluity.

In the Antarctic Circle, elves hide beneath crags of ice and build tiny fires until the escarpments splash into the sea.

I tear holes in the plaster walls.

Hank has my back.

No, he *has* it. He's holding it.

Ice cube trays until the distance.

No exceptions.

No skates.

Blue: a false cognate.

White: precisely how it sounds.

A boat with fat men.

Another dream of sanctioned loss.

The atoms, in love, collapse dramatically.

Point at the leaps of the free.

The land of the dead.

The ocean of _____.

Barnacles where I lent my blood.

Hank. Honey. Everything is gold for once.

We are unpursued.

The universe washes silently in our wake.

69°22'S 139°1'E

Every night we go around the table and give thanks. For the sky, for the snow, for the walls, for the slippers between us and the floor, for death, which will come soon enough, for the penguins, which at least are free—

In the Antarctic Circle thanks is bitterness, flung at what we don't have.

But tradition dies hard. We swivel our heads to take in the trappings of isolation and find that even they are sparse. Thanks for white. Thanks for winter. For the hole in the harpoon gun where the harpoon fits.

Thanks for the pits where our eyes go, for where breath travels, for the ducts that allow us to pass daily out of ourselves. Thanks for the rain, which high above us turns to snow. A shy gift lies in it: the certainty of eventual thaw.

LEFT BLANK

THIS PAGE

FREEZES OVER

65°16′S 103°6′E

First, the little toe. The big one next. Everything between, sufferance upon sufferance. Our pleasure shivers toward the cluttered sea.

My father told me once, while my mother shook her head: Tickling is nothing less than a gesture at the beyond. Do you hear that? God's salesman knocking at the door!

Hank shrieks and kicks at me. I know what his body is saying: There are more empty spaces than there are ways to fill. But that's an inborn fault. I don't stop. We don't have an uncle yet, and I'm not sorry.

Windows—we don't even have those. I'll stop when I can see the snow from inside the snow.

64°56'S 63°45'W

Our nerves have migrated to the southern cities. Populations have doubled: children of nerves.

The southern cities burn, smell like singed hair, torn car leather, speeches in favor of God forgotten and submitted to the ideology of distraction. Scroll and scroll.

If you know ink, remind your brother of it.

As his sister, your job is to collect the feelings and hold them under the snow. In time, they take on the characteristics of the uncharacteristically abandoned.

You like me, the feelings say, numb. You love me.

Do not believe them. In the sky they are driving to work, raining gas. Our synapses call out to each other the way mirrors call out to the lost. If the southern cities ever stop burning, their reward will be one mute century and a single year, following that, of nakedness.

But we can see what they are even without that last year: stalks of itching hay stuffed to fill a pair of white jeans.

74°35′S 111°0′W

The only way to get to the Dark Sector is to trudge. Titanium fills your cheeks. Formlessness tackles you and rubs snow in your eyes until you can see her. The dim promise of a new year lingers on the horizon but you'd rather someone cut a hole in the sun and fished you out, fed you to their family of five, and loved you for what you are, a mass of mostly bone. What flesh you have you owe to the winter. Your shape is the shape of stone. Your smile is someone else's whim. Your trust is back with Hank. He hovers above it, as brittle as a shoreline. The living room lifts him up with its thick gray fingers and plucks his ribs out, one by one. My hands are shaking at the thought of him suspended there. You think the cold is cold. Emptiness is only a beginning. Emptiness is a simple, ready receptacle.

66°15'S 121°30'E

All the earth's bats are right-side up, sleeping off the fight. They turn white in their hibernation. They won't speak and don't have the language. But they are somewhere near, I know.

Sweep the ceiling. Sweep the house. Sweep the table. Hank's hair. In our jumpsuits. Where we sweat. Our stone of a bed. I'll turn to the ice soon. Sweep it. Push away the sugar-snow until I find their den of warmth and dark, leathery life.

Still the bats won't come. Their peeping eyes are shut tight for once. They wait it out.

They know I'll cave first.

Hank risks glances at me. He's afraid to raise his hands, to warn me against the collapse we both know is calling.

I'll bite him. He knows I will.

Yes: That's the day the bats will wake.

66°13'S 110°36'E

I believe in Antarctica the way I believe in God's white palm. The way it brims with snow. The way the night ice is new to the morning ice. I believe that the moon shines down on a union, that somewhere in this tundra two are frozen into one.

Some day: I believe in that day.

In my life, a desperate insect drags lint across the living room floor.

Not a single memory fills me. I remember the beach. The flags we covered ourselves in. The beer we drank. No snow. The sky pretended to go on forever but stopped just beyond the eyes.

Forever was only an idea then, something someone said to someone and both quickly forgot. Waiting there for us.

THIS PAGE

DISCOVERS

THINNESS

A BREACH

90°0'S 0°0'W

The South Pole shudders at our approach.

In the Antarctic Circle, humans transmit like radio waves. Like lightning through water.

The South Pole is not in fact a pole.

The bald bottom of existence, shivering and doubting.

Darling—as in pola*rity*.

Without some deep-set hopes and/or beliefs, what is your purpose in coming?

The silence of the greatness of silence.

The long way out.

67°28'S 61°41'E

Wake to the glow of landing lights arranged in an A-OK— Air-traffic ghosts pioneering a runway site for faith— Our savior touching down at the helm of a 787—

You're going to be fine, you say. You're translucent already.

An accidental harpoon-swing— The quick drop of the sun— An unattached wind at just the wrong moment—

Nobody is to blame for these things. Your gauze, you keep on saying, looks as healthy as sickness gets.

I can see it now: We'll march down the runway stairs and scoop up armfuls of soil, spread it on our bones.

I told you once that God meant for us to connect the dots.

I take it back. My innermost organs, bright and heavy, are praying for collapse to deliver them.

78°30'S 61°0'W

Far too saccharine, his ten fingers on my neck. Hank's massage pulps my muscles. His optimism picks at me.

We'll make it, he says. We'll make it. Always: What is there to make?

Besides love, which he pursues in the style of a lion after a lioness trying to tend to her cubs. A perpetual motion into and away. A length of twine tied tightly to the mind.

The products right beside the process, staring at it wide-eyed. Wholly unaware of the swollen months that fall between.

77°7′S 158°1′W

I want *sorry*. I want your white palms. I want your faulty canals, your half-headed promises, your veins. I want *trust*, though I cannot trust when I see only your tracks, and the tracks are only an image, and the image is only two clasped hands, cold and dry like the sky hurrying toward us. I want *miserable*. I want *ache*. Take those tracks and paint with them and we will talk. I want a humid rhythm. I want *fear*, yours and mine, hairless pallid skin, hole in the cranium for thoughtless squares of sky. You have been waiting all this time and now I am answering you: This is what I want, your arrow, your bow, your bullseye, tied together and buried and excavated and burned to make water.

I won't touch you. I won't touch you even if you fall in.

64°43′S 62°41′W

The symbols cry out to us:

Xs in the eyes.

Blood-spotted pillow.

An eagle's caw.

The endless sun.

A window cracked from cold.

A seal outside it, barking.

This means the end is near, says Hank.

No. It means the end has come and already left.

THIS PAGE
IS A CONTINENT
THIS PAGE
IS A DOOR

64°44'S 62°37'W

Once we rise we rise quickly, as if a massacre is occurring under our feet. The ground fills the window. Touches us from a distance. Becomes clear in its blankness, no longer needing to lie.

The long plane rights itself. For the first time in years, we survive.

We dream: We've already been saved. The snow outside is our blanket. In other landscapes, howitzers roll across hills and lock in place, preparing to leave huge furrows. The Antarctic Circle heaves and contracts around us.

Its touch is bigger than anyone knew. It strides into outer space. Strokes the stars. Calls them by our names.

75°37'S 132°25'W

I had plenty of coping mechanisms. Swimming. Hank. French food, which I could eat because I swam.

Try swimming in the Antarctic Circle. It's called looking for a place to fall.

There's nothing to cope *with*. I never knew how badly I needed my unhappiness.

If I had known, I would have gathered it up in small, heavy glass beads.

Woven them into my underwear. Never sat again.

69°57′S 38°45′E

Hank is filled to the brim with neutrinos. We touch metal but sugar-snow still pulls earthly on us, reminding us that something else is out there, alive. Glacier walls. Grinning bearded ghosts pacing like Americans. Flagpoles and boots strew the tundra, spit out by the ice. Long live the light.

Long live the darkness, raining flagpoles and boots. Sad long-haired men pace the sky in Norwegian, dip below the dunes and seem for a moment dead. Then their crowns return, same as the bitter snow, and turn to bodies. They are magnetic, wooden, pull us toward them and push us away at once. They stop at our door and knock. The sound of their padded fists is the sound of a glacier refusing to crumble.

77°31′S 167°9′E

In the Antarctic Circle, memory is a lampshade, softening the light.
The snow is a massive reflector, blinding you.

No need for cleaning products in a world where no bacteria
survive.

Cast off. Let me know what it's like on top of the blue expanse.

The parade. Shadowless.

If you can see the mountains, touch them for me.

Thus, the polar explorers do not perform an innocent quest, and their nostalgia for earlier epochs is not sufficient to redeem them. As a result of their non-human encounters, they are forced to turn inward, finding in the incoherence and cruelty of the landscape an objective correlative for their alienation and solitude.

—Nicoletta Brazzelli

I shall not go in search of it. . . and am only sorry that in searching after those imaginary Lands, I have spent so much time. . .

—Captain James Cook

I live in a house that is your name but I forget your name. The grass out front is as green as snow.

The single breadth in me reaches across the outer breadth, an infinite expanse of cubic desire. But I can only hold breadth for so long.

After, I lean on my walls. They attribute meaning to the skin.

They pull back when I pull away. Memory is short. There is something between me and it.

Something in the shape of the continent. A bulge and a reach. It is blank, but it is there.

NOTES

Page 3. Lize-Marié van der Watt and Sandra Swart. "The Whiteness of Antarctica: Race and South Africa's Antarctic History." In *Antarctica and the Humanities,* edited by Peder Roberts, Lize-Marié van der Watt, and Adrian Howkins. Palgrave Macmillan, 2016.

Page 7. Edgar Allan Poe. *The Narrative of Arthur Gordon Pym of Nantucket.* Penguin, 1999.
    Toni Morrison. *Playing in the Dark: Whiteness and the Literary Imagination.* Vintage, 1993.

Page 43. Elizabeth Leane. *Antarctica in Fiction: Imaginative Narratives of the Far South.* Cambridge University Press, 2012.
    Elena Glasberg. *Antarctica as Cultural Critique: The Gendered Politics of Scientific Exploration and Climate Change.* Palgrave MacMillan, 2012.

Page 49. Apsley Cherry-Garrard. *The Worst Journey in the World.* Penguin, 2005.

Page 83. Nicoletta Brazzelli. "A Symbolic Geography of the Ice: Apsley Cherry-Garrard, The Worst Journey in the World and Modernity." In *The Politics and Poetics of Displacement,* edited by Massimo Bacigalupo and Luisa Villa. Campanotto, 2011.
    J.C. Beaglehole, editor. *The Journals of Captain James Cook on his Voyages of Discovery: Volume II: The Voyage of the Resolution and Adventure 1772-1775.* Routledge, 2017. I came upon this quotation from Cook's journals as an epigraph in another work: Siobhan Carroll. *An Empire of Air and Water: Uncolonizable Space in the British Imagination, 1750-1850.* University of Pennsylvania Press, 2015.

ACKNOWLEDGMENTS

Thank you to the editors of the following venues, who published portions of this manuscript in their first iterations: *Bateau, Birdfeast, elsewhere, Juked, Gargoyle Magazine, Heavy Feather Review, LEVELER, Passages North, Phantom, Poor Claudia, Prelude, Quarterly West, Requited, Salt Hill, Territory, wildness,* and Greying Ghost Press.

Thank you to Keith Scribner, Marjorie Sandor, Jennifer Richter, Susan Jackson Rodgers, Karen Holmberg, Elena Passarello, and Nick Dybek, all of whom guided me as a writer while I wrote the first draft of this book; to my friends and colleagues at Oregon State University, for their helpful feedback on this and other writing; and to Oregon State University, which provided the means for me to live while I was writing.

Thank you to Yona Harvey for making my dream come true by selecting this book; to Julie Carr and Maryse Meijer for their generous words; to Joel Coggins for the design; and to Christine Stroud for her patience, insight, and commitment to bringing *In the Antarctic Circle* to life.

I will be forever grateful to my parents for their unfading belief in me, and to Thirii, without whose love and reassurance this book would never have found a home.

ABOUT THE AUTHOR

Dennis James Sweeney's writing has appeared in *Crazyhorse, Five Points, Ninth Letter, The New York Times,* and *The Southern Review,* among others, as well as in four chapbooks of poetry and prose. A Small Press Editor of *Entropy* and a former Fulbright fellow in Malta, he has an MFA from Oregon State University and a PhD from the University of Denver. Originally from Cincinnati, he lives in Amherst, Massachusetts.

NEW AND FORTHCOMING RELEASES

No One Leaves the World Unhurt by John Foy
Winner of the 2020 Donald Justice Poetry Prize
selected by J. Allyn Rosser

Lucky Wreck: Anniversary Edition by Ada Limón

Creep Love by Michael Walsh

The Dream Women Called by Lori Wilson

"American" Home by Sean Cho A.
Winner of the 2020 Autumn House Chapbook Prize
selected by Danusha Laméris

Under the Broom Tree by Natalie Homer

Molly by Kevin Honold
Winner of the 2020 Autumn House Fiction Prize
selected by Dan Chaon

The Animal Indoors by Carly Inghram
Winner of the 2020 CAAPP Book Prize
selected by Terrance Hayes

speculation, n. by Shayla Lawz
Winner of the 2020 Autumn House Poetry Prize
selected by Ilya Kaminsky

All Who Belong May Enter by Nicholas Ward
Winner of the 2020 Autumn House Nonfiction Prize
selected by Jaquira Díaz

For our full catalog please visit: www.autumnhouse.org